# Marriage Wisdom

## FOR HIM

# Marriage Wisdom

## FOR HIM

## A 31 DAY DEVOTIONAL
### FOR BUILDING A BETTER MARRIAGE

## MATTHEW L. JACOBSON

LOYAL
ARTS MEDIA

© 2017 by Matthew L. Jacobson

Published by
Loyal Arts Media
P.O. Box 1414
Bend, OR 97709
loyartsmedia.com

Printed in the United States of America

Cover painting by Lance Austin Olsen
Cover design by Jamie Drouin

ISBN 978-1-929125-53-1 (paperback)

# Table of Contents

# Introduction

This book is filled with practical wisdom from a biblical perspective for a fantastic marriage that's deeply satisfying. It's concise and direct. It's also powerless to bring about positive change unless . . . unless you are willing to not only read these words but purpose to apply them in your marriage. For those who do, something awesome awaits you and your wife.

MLJ

# 1

# Increase Her Desire

*Lovingly meet her needs and*
*she'll make sure you don't have any.*

*M*any men spend years wishing their wives would be more responsive. *Why doesn't she show more interest in, or desire for, sex with me?* Frustration builds. Not only is a sense of deprivation gnawing away – emotional distance between you grows. And then there's the anger . . . like molten lava that is bubbling up to the surface.

You know you're being short-changed . . . that's the way you feel, isn't it? And it makes you mad when you think about it.

A simple and powerful truth is needlessly missed by so many men.

. . . And, what is that truth?

If you're not giving at all, if you're giving little or just giving to get, she'll continue to withhold herself from you.

She wants to be yours completely, but she doesn't want to be used or taken for granted. That's how she feels when you expect regular sex but don't take care to consider what her heart needs and desires.

Yes, she desires to be with you, *but that desire doesn't begin in bed.*

Loving consideration of her needs is what she needs, in her soul, to feel loved and to offer herself with dignity and joy to you. So don't give to get. Give to love. Let love, not self-consideration, be the driving force behind your care of her.

What are her needs? (Sounds like a conversation for date night, doesn't it?) She'll love you for wanting to know what she needs, and she'll love you better for following through on what you learn from her – not to get what you want, but for truly wanting her to feel known and cherished by you.

Rhino horn, raw oysters, stylish Italian clothes and expensive cologne – in this world, there are many competing claims for "best aphrodisiac." But a wise man knows that casting about for the latest new idea to make her want you is as easy as a walk in the park, holding hands, being truly interested in her as a person, and communicating to her that you care about her needs . . . that you truly want her.

Meeting her needs might include making sure she has

had an uninterrupted afternoon nap, dealing with that easy-to-ignore household task she's asked you to do about a zillion times, ensuring she has some "me" time, or taking the kids for six hours straight on a Saturday so she can go somewhere and breathe.

The "what" of meeting her needs depends on the "who."

To whom are you married?

Every woman is different in what says "love" to her – remember that date night conversation? – but there is an important way in which every wife is the same. She is a person who needs to feel love that says, "I am here to nurture you and to care for your needs, not just to get what I want."

The Bible says, "Let each of you look out not only for his own interests, but also for the interests of others." (Philippians 2:4)

Marriage . . . there's no better place to apply this wisdom.

*Dear Lord,*

*Please help me to consider my wife's needs and the desires of her heart in a way that communicates love to her. Help me speak and interact with her in a way that demonstrates how much I value her as the unique person You created her to be. And Lord, even if she doesn't always respond to me in the way I desire, help me to only respond in love and to love her unconditionally, as You have loved me.*

*In Jesus' name, amen.*

## Ask Your Wife:

"What do you need? Is there a way I could help you rest, a special way I could spend time with you, or a chore you would really like me to do immediately?"

Notes

Notes

# 2

# No Hidden Sin

*Never be found in places or doing things
you would be ashamed to have
your spouse discover by chance.*

Temptation – it's everywhere. But it's worse than that. It's not just "out there." Our flesh naturally responds to – even desires – the filth that is dished up on every side in this porn-soaked, sex-driven world. Let's be honest: our baser self, our unfettered flesh, is capable of just about anything.

The Marine Corp motto is *semper fidelis* – always faithful. What would happen if marines were only faithful 90% of the time and the other 10% they were treasonous? It wouldn't take any more than that to destroy this country.

The same is true for marriage. A little unfaithfulness goes a long, long way.

Do you treat your wife with honor when no one is looking? Are you *semper fidelis?*

When temptation offers a little something here . . . a morsel there . . . ask yourself, "If my wife were here, right now, watching me in this moment, would I feel ashamed?"

Then say no to the temptation and walk on. Stop looking. Don't click. It's the exact same action you would want from her in similar circumstances.

For the Christian, there's a whole other level of concern. Never mind what your wife thinks; what does God think about you skulking around with the morals of an alley rat?

Do you find yourself thinking, "It's only a little bit . . . only a little sin"?

If you've convinced yourself God is good with a little sin, you had better think again.

> "Do not be deceived. Neither fornicators [illicit sex – the root word of "pornography"], nor idolaters [a worshiper of false gods, one who covets], nor adulterers [which includes the idea of faithlessness to God] . . . will inherit the kingdom of God." (1 Corinthians 6:9-10)

How destructive it would be to have your wife catch you delving where no man – married or otherwise – should go. You don't want to crush her heart, do you?

How much worse it would be to discover, too late, that

your "little" sin that you refused to repent of and forsake had separated you from God, forever.

Say no to temptation before it becomes a second look, then a thought pattern, then a decision, and then an action. Keep your mind undefiled and your marriage bed will follow suit.

*Dear Lord,*

*There are sexual temptations on every side and in front of me every day. I often feel under attack. The enemy is very real but I know that doesn't have to matter if I keep my eyes on You. Help me believe and walk in the truth — that You have made an escape for me in the face of every temptation. I am not weak as the enemy wants me to think, but strong because I am indwelt by Your Holy Spirit. Help me to walk in the victory You won for me at the cross. Help me to be faithful to You and to my wife every moment of every day. From this time forward, may I honor You and her all the days of my life.*

*In Jesus' name, amen.*

## ASK YOUR WIFE:

"Do you realize that I face temptation often? I commit to you to stand strong against temptation, in the grace God gives me. Would you do something for me? It would mean so much to me to have your prayers for my strength in this area: would you pray for me?"

# Notes

# Notes

# 3

# Kiss Her Like It's the Last Time, Every Time

*The years will pass, but she will never tire
of the truth contained in a sincere kiss.
A wise husband kisses his wife every day!*

Life has a subtle but effective way of sweeping away passion from marriage, leaving a struggling, flickering flame where once a fire burned with intense heat.

Never was a fire more easily rekindled.

Whenever you kiss, kiss her like it matters for eternity.

A little focus and very little effort can make a massive impact on your wife's perception of the intensity of your love for her. In the morning when you part, during the weekend before lunch, at night helping with dishes (or whatever you do), kiss her with passion. Make her believe you mean it from deep inside. You're the co-star in her love story. No wife can maintain intensity and passion on her own. Unless she's hurt and her heart is closed to her husband, every wife – no matter how old – still desires to be kissed like she was on her wedding day. You're the leading man in this epic, so lead with an unforgettable kiss, every time.

How do you do that?

Start by holding her a little closer and adding five seconds to your next kiss. Of course, you won't go wrong adding to that baseline!

Now, some guys just don't (or refuse to) get it. If you're kissing to get something – like . . . oh, I don't know . . . sex, for instance? – then you just blew it. She'll know you're kissing to get. She'll know you're kissing for you, not for her.

Never kiss to get. Kiss to inspire. Don't kiss for you. Kiss for her.

You'll be amazed at where this "road less traveled" will take you.

*Dear Lord,*

*Sometimes I let the pressures and busyness of life cause me to forget how intensely my wife needs me to love her with a sincere kiss. Lord, this request feels a little odd but please help me to focus on becoming the kind of kisser that leaves no doubt in my wife's mind that she is deeply loved, truly understanding that she is important to me. Help her to feel that when I am kissing her, I am sincerely giving myself to her.*

*In Jesus' name, amen.*

## ASK YOUR WIFE:

Look at your wife in love and ask her if you can practice this devotional material right now. Remember, kiss to inspire.

Notes

# 4
## Express Gratitude

*An ounce of gold in a poor country*
*and a little gratitude in marriage are alike.*
*They both go a long way.*

Many a wife feels unappreciated by the most important person in her life. Is your wife one of them?

The question isn't whether you are grateful for your wife. The question is, does she *know* you are grateful for her . . . does she *feel* your gratitude in her heart?

Many husbands are ready and willing to tell everyone else how amazing their wife is, how grateful they are for her, and how much she is appreciated.

And just as many wives would be stunned speechless if they ever heard such declarations from their husbands with their own ears.

When was the last time you took your woman in your arms, looked deeply into her eyes, and told her three things you truly appreciate about her?

But maybe you're one of those husbands who isn't really all that grateful. Many husbands don't know how good they have it. Here's the truth: you're married to a good woman who does a lot for you.

Sometimes we're so enveloped by blessings that we lose perspective and cease to be grateful. How can a husband tell if he has become ungrateful? Easy, just ask your wife. "Hey Babe, do you feel that I'm grateful for you and for all you do?"

Many wives would be shocked that the question was even asked, so congrats for a strong start, husband! The question is, are you prepared for the answer?

What's more . . . are you prepared to be humble and to change, if the answer is any degree of no?

Gratitude answers a deep need in a wife's heart to be truly valued.

She wants to know: "Does what I do around here matter to him? Does it even register in his thinking?"

It takes so very little (not that we should offer our gratitude in small doses) for most wives to feel appreciated. Start today. Find something every day this week (and beyond) to express gratitude for. Words are so powerful; use them. Open your mouth and say something affirming to her. It's not difficult.

There's nothing like gratitude to open hearts and deepen relationships. You want to be appreciated – so does your wife . . . from the most important person in her life.

Gratitude is powerful "glue" in the marriage relationship. Be wise and apply it sincerely in yours.

*Dear Lord,*

*Thank You for my amazing wife. She is truly a gift from You, but I know sometimes I act in a way that causes her not to feel like the gift she is. Please help me to express, through words and actions, how genuinely I appreciate her and how grateful I am for her — for the many things she does, but especially for who she is, as a wonderful person You've blessed me to share my life with. Thank You for giving her to me.*

*In Jesus' name, amen.*

## ASK YOUR WIFE:

"Do you feel that I am grateful for who you are as a person? Is there something that you work really hard at that you feel moves under my radar?"

Notes

# Notes

# 5
## Fill Her Emotional Reservoir

*A pitcher of water and a wife are alike.*
*Both pour out until they are empty.*
*The wife refills the pitcher. Who will refill*
*the wife? Is there a wise man in the house?*

I t's easy to think your wife is just like you, that she can soldier on day after day, going for weeks without meaningful, loving care. It's also easy to fall into the pattern of thinking, *My wife is emotionally needy – she's constantly wanting my time and attention, even though I give her my attention all the time.*

First of all, recognize that your "all the time" and her "all the time" are two very different things. It doesn't always work out this way, but in most marriages, the guy needs far less connection time and communication than his wife does. Her needs are just different; she is made differently.

She's pouring out her care – her heart and soul – in relationships all day, every day. It's what her engine runs on. In large measure, the "pouring in" must come from you, the most important human relationship she will ever have.

Yes, you took her out last week (great move!), and that connection and the sex you've continued to enjoy with her since then has kept you "tanked up." You don't need anything more. But for her, last week was . . . well . . . last week. And sex since then – even though she enjoyed being with you – isn't the only thing she needs to fill her emotional tank.

No woman can remain emotionally and relationally fulfilled on past expressions of your love, commitment, and care.

For her, the past connection was great, and she appreciated it, but she needs a present connection with you – today, this week, and next. It's how she's wired.

Think of it this way. How often do the two of you have sex? For the average couple, it's two to three times per week. You may have more or less, but wherever you fall on the scale, if you have a healthy sex life and feel that things are positive, you're basically happy, right?

When a husband is happy with his sex life, he tends to think his wife is happy, too. It's easy to think that just because your needs are fulfilled, so are your wife's. After all, there haven't been any emotional outbursts or blow-ups recently. The house has been running smoothly. Everything must be great, right? Thinking like this is an oversight, and guys make this mistake all the time.

Just because you're married to a good woman and she isn't freaking out doesn't mean her heart has been well tended and her emotional needs have been met. And here's one you can take to the bank: sex may fill most of your emotional needs, but sex will never fulfill all your wife's emotional needs.

Sometimes we need a jolt to get it.

What if your wife came to you and said this? "From now on, we're going to have sex once every three months. I don't need or want it any more than that."

*What? Four times a year?!!*

You'd be bugged – angry, even – wouldn't you? You are wired for sex and this deprivation would make you crazy. After all, it's an important element to how you are connected to her at a heart level.

Emotional connection through meaningful, interested conversation and careful attention to things that make her feel loved is every bit as important to her as sex is to you. It's how she is connected to you at a heart level.

She's not just a wife; she's a woman. She is pouring out constantly to you, to the kids (if you have them), to extended family, and to friends. She needs you – she's counting on you – to be engaged, to care for her at a heart level. *That* is what fills her emotional tank.

The more you seek to be connected at a heart level, the more she will desire you and enjoy being with you physically.

*Dear Lord,*

*It's difficult to remember that my wife doesn't think like I do and has different needs than I do. Help me to remember that. If I start to continue on through my week, forgetting this fact, please prompt me to change my thoughts and behavior toward her, so she will receive from me what she needs to be her best. Lord, life is so busy, and it's easy to give myself a pass in this area but I don't want to do that going forward, and I humbly ask Your help in making sure my wife's emotional tank is always "full." Thank You.*

*In Jesus' name, amen.*

## Ask Your Wife:

Tell your wife how important it is for you to make sure her emotional tank is full. Ask her, "Are there any things I do that make you feel like your needs are met and that you are connected with me? If you were going to add three things to that list, what would they be?"

# Notes

# 6
## No Public Correction

*To swats at wasps and the man who corrects
his wife in public are alike —
eventually, they'll both get stung.*

It never fails. Get the gang together for a summer picnic
and before long, someone is swatting wasps off the
burgers . . . Everyone knows how this story ends; it
won't take long before someone gets stung.

Your wife isn't a wasp, but you'll turn her into one by
being careless with her dignity in public, embarrassing her
by repeatedly correcting her in front of others.

"She was wrong about that. I was just setting the record
straight."

Congratulations, you were right. And dominating your
wife in public with your "rightness" has such great long-
term results, doesn't it?

The core issue isn't who was technically correct. What was actually happening was that you were demeaning her, making her feel small. If embarrassment and engendering disrespect was the goal, mission accomplished.

The party is over, everyone is gone, and the venom starts to fly. Maybe it started before people left, and her pain started to show with some snide remarks and an increasing chill factor. Maybe you're married to a woman who just gets silent – until later . . .

Either way, your "rightness" is what created this environment.

It's all so unnecessary. Just don't correct her (put her down) in public. If something absolutely must be addressed, wait until you're in private. In marriage, there's almost nothing that can't wait until you're alone.

So, what is the biggest problem here?

Truth . . . without love.

The Bible doesn't just instruct us to speak the truth; it tells us to speak the truth *in love*. (Ephesians 4:15)

Part of loving your wife is being big enough not to "score points" at your wife's expense in public. Wait until later to share your feelings. After all, she would like to be corrected in public about as much as you do.

A prayer for those who struggle with this problem:

*Dear Lord,*

*Please forgive me for dishonoring You and my wife in this manner. I desire to change my disrespectful, degrading behavior and ask that You check my spirit when I'm tempted to speak in this way. Thank You for working in my life and bringing the needed understanding and the change that You desire in me. I pray my wife will forgive me and truly see a change in me.*

*In Jesus' name, amen.*

A prayer for those who don't struggle with this problem:

*Dear Lord,*

*Help me never to develop the habit of correcting my wife when we are with others. I pray that she always feels honored by me in public. I also pray that if I observe this habit in other husbands that You would give me the boldness to correct my brother in love.*

*In Jesus' name, amen.*

# ASK YOUR WIFE:

"Have I ever corrected you in the presence of others? If so, I'm so sorry for that. Will you please forgive me? And please know, I'm determined to stop doing this!"

# Notes

# Notes

# 7

# Give Her Proof She Is Your Priority

*He who is more concerned with the feelings of others than the feelings and needs of his wife is like the man who dumps water on a fire and expects it to still keep him warm at night.*

She can take a lot, this woman you're married to. She knows she's married to a good man . . . a man who loves people, who puts himself out there for others, who will deny himself over and over again to help friends and family.

It's one of the reasons she married you. She loves that about you. You genuinely enjoy helping others . . . even if there is a steep cost to your time, energy, and sometimes money.

You're a good man.

But, there's something good men forget when they're busy staying up late, getting up early, taking Saturdays to help others, postponing vacations one more day to give a hand to someone, or canceling dinner plans with their woman because a friend just called with a serious need.

There is something *you* are forgetting.

This frenzy of needs will *never* stop! And you aren't the only one paying the price for your readiness to drop everything and meet the needs of others. Your wife is paying that price, right alongside you.

How many times have you changed plans to help someone else? How many times did you come home late (and leave her alone) because of commitments you made? How many times did you meet someone else's needs before you met your wife's needs for time and connection with you?

You are not your own. When the Bible says, "The two shall become one" (Mark 10:8), it's not just a reference to what happens when the lights go out in the bedroom. Every decision you make to meet the needs of others potentially compromises the time, attention, and connection that your wife desires with you. Your decisions affect her every bit as much as they affect you.

You're a good guy, and she's a good woman, which means that she won't overreact the first few times this happens. But the light in her heart will begin to dim as you attempt to meet the needs of everyone else but neglect hers.

Left uncorrected, your marriage bed will eventually grow cold – not all at once but by degrees – until you'll discover you've extinguished the sparkle in her eye and the life in her heart.

Your wife should have first place in your heart, and merely saying those words proves nothing. Actions are where your priorities are seen and felt. Meet her needs first, and you'll discover she'll practically kick you out the door to fulfill your desire to "be there" for others.

Spare yourself a discontented wife by saying no to old patterns. Choose to mature in this area, and recognize you are not your own.

*Dear Lord,*

*I do like to help others but I want to make certain I don't neglect my wife when I'm doing "all that good." Help me to realize that she is paying the cost of my service to others. I pray she will never feel "second fiddle," no matter how good my intentions may be in helping others. Lord, You've commanded me to love her as Christ loved the church. I pray that my wife feels this commitment by how I order my priorities from now on.*

*In Jesus' name, amen.*

## ASK YOUR WIFE:

"Do you feel like you are my number one priority, or do you feel like just one priority among many? When have I made you feel like you're in second place when it comes to meeting the needs of others?"

# Notes

Notes

# 8
# Never Steal from Her

*He who has sex with himself
is brother to him who steals.
Theft always leaves an empty room.*

ou're alone for a few . . . she's in the other part of the house, away for the day, out for the evening, sleeping, distracted . . . the main thing is, you're alone . . . .

*Hey, I'll just fire one off in the shower . . . no harm, no foul.*

It's okay, right? After all, you want sex far more than she does (in the typical relationship . . . there are exceptions) so, why not have a quick one and not bother her?

Or, maybe you're one of those guys who seldom has sex with your wife (I'm tired, stressed, etc., you tell her again, and again) but often party by yourself without her knowing.

Whatever the reason, it's not important because what she doesn't know won't hurt her, right?

And then she walks in, throws back the shower curtain . . . and, there you are. Caught red-handed. "Babe . . . I was, uh . . . just thinking of you, really."

Right.

How do you feel then? Like Adam running around the Garden of Eden looking for fig leaves?

But you told yourself it was no big deal. So, why are you covered with embarrassment and shame? If it was all okay, why is your wife filled with hurt and anger? Why did she leave the room disgusted, feeling . . . gross?

*No harm, no foul, remember?*

But there is harm because marching to the beat of your own drum is foul.

You told yourself you can masturbate without consequences (as long as she doesn't find out) but, in fact, it was all a convenient lie so you could get what you want. You *knew* from the start it was wrong, which is why you became a deceiver in the first place.

What has really happened here? First of all, you're being secretive – sneaky – behind your wife's back. *Can't let her find out.* From where did the idea come that having private orgasms apart from the knowledge and involvement of your wife was okay?

It's absurd. And, sneaking around your own home

trying to keep your sexual activity hidden from your wife makes you a liar.

No healthy marriage relationship has secrets, especially sexual secrets.

So, you've lied to your wife. You've also betrayed her, pretending to be something you're not: faithful. Masturbation is unfaithfulness. It's sexual sin, against your wife.

Masturbation is theft from, lying to, and betrayal of your wife. Your secret sex life is robbing your wife of what is rightfully hers.

The Bible is such an interesting book when it comes to the subject of sex. The New Testament was written in the context of cultures that had little to no respect for women, especially wives. For the most part, they were owned, like property. Along comes the Bible and says that a wife has just as much right to her husband's body as the husband has to his wife's body.

Husbands and wives are directly instructed not to withhold from each other. 1 Corinthians 7:3-5 says (paraphrased), "The husband should fulfill his wife's sexual needs, and likewise the wife, her husband's. For the wife does not have authority over her own body, but the husband does. Likewise, the husband does not have authority over his own body, but the wife does. Do not deprive one another [not have sex on a regular basis], except perhaps by agreement for a limited time, that you may devote yourselves to prayer; but then come together again, so that Satan may not tempt you because of your lack of self-control."

So, when you decided to go solo, you withheld – robbed – your wife of what is rightfully hers. Your body parts are not exclusively yours to do with what you want – which is why you feel shame when you get caught. The two of you are one and husbands can choose to care for what belongs to their wives – their bodies – with honor or dishonor.

Choose honor, even when it's difficult. That's what makes it honor.

The thing about leading a double life is, sooner or later, the light is going to shine in and expose what's really there. If you don't want to be ashamed of yourself – if you don't want to betray your wife and have her lose respect for you – receive the truth that your body and all its parts belong to her. She has every right to know where they've been and how they are being used.

A prayer for those who struggle with the sin of masturbation:

*Dear Lord,*

*I confess my sin before You. I've believed and have told myself lies, to justify what my flesh desires. I'm done with all that. I repent of my sin. Please forgive me. I've sinned against You and in so doing, I've sinned against my wife. Help me to have the courage to confess to her. I don't know how she will respond, but I pray she will know I am truly sorry and have genuinely repented of my sin. May I never, ever, keep anything from You or from my wife, again.*

*In Jesus' name, amen.*

A prayer for those who don't struggle with the sin of masturbation:

*Dear Lord,*

*I'm grateful I haven't struggled in this area, but as You know, there are many other areas in which I do struggle. I know a prideful spirit will only bring me down, so I humbly give thanks for strength in this area but recognize that I am always a target of the enemy. You've given me the strength to choose the right way to live. I pray I use the strength You've given me, to honor You and my wife 100% of the time. Thank You.*

*In Jesus' name, amen.*

## TELL YOUR WIFE:

Come clean if you have sin to confess. Tell her what you've been doing. Acknowledge that you've been deceiving her and robbing her. Ask her to forgive you. Then, start living a different way.

# Notes

Notes

# 9
# Be Her Friend

*As water is to a garden,*
*so friendship is to a great marriage*

*He's my friend.* Is that the thought that comes to the mind of your wife when she thinks of you and your relationship?

If so, fantastic! You are among the few and are providing a good example of what marriage can be.

Friendship in marriage doesn't just happen on its own, which is why many wives in basically stable marriages feel alone or distant, longing for *something more* that feels just beyond their grasp.

Here is where many wives are:

► Things are functioning, the wheels are on the wagon, the family is getting fed – *check.*

▶ We're connecting physically, things are pretty regular – *check*.

▶ Our friendship . . . well, I wish it could be deeper, more of a priority . . .

Are you purposefully pursuing your wife as your friend? Not for sex, but for her? Does she know in her heart that you *really* like her?

Friendship isn't complicated. It's just a process of accumulating lots of moments together that you both enjoy. The "accumulating" part takes intention, purpose, and focus.

Does your wife feel that you enjoy spending time with her, or does she sense that it is about checking the box of marital obligation for you – before you get back to the football game or whatever it is that you value more than her?

There is no great garden without water and there's no great marriage without friendship.

Pursue greatness . . . pursue friendship with your wife. She'll love you all the more for it.

*Dear Lord,*

*Thank You for the amazing gift of my wife. I pray that I will be the best friend to her that she imagined her husband would be. Help me to grow in this area. Give me understanding as to how to cultivate an ever deepening friendship with this awesome woman! Thank You.*

*In Jesus' name, amen.*

## ASK YOUR WIFE:

"Do you know that I like you? That I like being with you? Do you feel like we are excellent friends? What specific things do you feel would help us deepen our friendship?"

Notes

# 10

# Speak Kind Words Every Day

*A winter sun and a kind word are alike:
they melt frozen places.*

$S$omething happened and you find yourselves at an impasse. She's not communicating, and her heart is as cold as stone on a winter's day.

Rocky, stony places: every marriage – even a great marriage – has them. Have you come to that patch of difficult terrain in your marriage?

*How did we get here?*

It's time to unleash the power of warm sincerity with kind, soft words. This isn't the time for precision in an argument. This isn't the time to parse what was said. This isn't the time to make sure the "right" thing gets set straight.

This is the time for kind, soft words.

No amount of emotional heat will thaw the frozen places of the heart. No force of argument can or will move that stone.

Only kindness, in the form of soft words, can bring warmth where the frigid winds of hurt are blowing. "A soft answer turns away wrath." (Proverbs 15:1)

You raised your voice just a little. She says you were yelling.

*Yelling? I was just speaking with a little intensity, that's it. Yelling? She can't be serious.*

But, she is serious. It was yelling to her. That's how it *felt* to her, regardless of the actual decibels. You're likely a lot more forceful than you realize. All your insistence, force, and logic won't move her. What if you poured all that strength and force into gentleness, kindness, and softness?

Be among that rare group of husbands who have learned the immense power of soft, kind words. They will move mountains of ice.

*Dear Lord,*

*Please do Your work in my heart and mind so the next time we hit a stony patch, she will receive from me gentle tones and healing words, instead of harshness. Fill me with Your Spirit, to walk in a pleasing manner to You and in a safe, gentle, kind manner with the wife You gave to me.*

*In Jesus' name, amen.*

## ASK YOUR WIFE:

(Gently) "When you think of how I communicate to you, do you think: 'strong, forceful, harsh, opinionated, argumentative' or do you think, 'thoughtful, gentle, loving, soft, caring?'"

# Notes

# 11

# Stay Focused on Where YOU Need to Change

*When a man purposes to be a husband worthy of the woman of his dreams, it's amazing how she appears — before his very eyes — in the wife God gave him.*

Focusing on the failures and needed growth of your wife is as natural as breathing. How clearly you see her faults and shortcomings. If she would only do more of . . . if she wasn't so . . . if she would stop doing . . . .

The Bible reminds us that we ourselves often have far more "issues" than our wives.

Luke 6:42 says, ". . . how can you say to your brother,

'Brother, let me remove the speck that is in your eye,' when you yourself do not see the plank that is in your own eye? Hypocrite! First remove the plank from your own eye, and then you will see clearly to remove the speck that is in your brother's eye."

You'd much rather focus on the "speck" in your wife's eye, wouldn't you?

Instead of allowing yourself to focus on the ways you'd like her to change – the ways you (pridefully) think she doesn't measure up – how about taking a biblical approach? Reflect on how you can better live up to the standards to which you are holding your wife.

Negative thoughts about your wife are like a spiral, and they only go one direction: down. Nothing positive or productive will come from them.

The next time you are inclined to have judgmental thoughts toward your wife, ask yourself instead, "In what areas do I need to improve?"

When we change our focus to the areas we need to grow in, it's amazing how our perspective changes toward our wives.

*Dear Lord,*

*You warn me not to be a hypocrite, and yet I often forget that and see only the faults in others and, in all honesty, especially in my wife. Instead of focusing on the many areas in my own life that need to change, I'm too quick to point out my wife's shortcomings. I want to mature in this, and I ask that You help me to hear Your Word and refocus on my own need for growth when the inclination to criticize my wife arises.*

*In Jesus' name, amen.*

## ASK YOUR WIFE:

"Do you feel that I have a critical spirit toward you? Do you feel I often see shortcomings instead of your strengths? If so, I deeply desire to make a change. I never want you to feel this way again."

# Notes

# 12

# No Angry Outbursts Against Her

*Don't let the sun go down on your wrath.*
*In fact, don't be wrathful at all*
*or the sun will go down on a spouse sleeping alone.*

How do you like sleeping alone?

Not so much?

Then don't let wrath – uncontrolled anger – have a place in your relationship or you'll find yourself with the blankets all to yourself . . . on the couch.

An angry, explosive spirit is repulsive to women, but it's worse than that. It's unacceptable to God. It's sin, pure and simple.

I'm going to share a way ahead for angry husbands but

first, I want to make sure you understand the Bible's take on this. In brief: you are a fool if you give full vent to your anger.

Fool? Isn't that a little harsh? No, it isn't. It's exactly what the Bible calls the man who blasts others with his anger. Proverbs 29:11 says, "A fool vents all his feelings."

Do what the world says and what your flesh desires in the moment of emotional intensity . . . and be a fool. Not only that but you'll be a destructive fool. Keep it up and eventually, you'll also be a lonely fool.

Here are three incredibly encouraging facts about expressing anger to your spouse:

1.  It doesn't have to happen.
2.  It's a choice.
3.  With God's help, you can control your response to whatever happens.

We sometimes act as if our anger is out of our control – just sneaks up on us and pounces on the situation. But this isn't true. Anger *is* within your control. You choose to allow yourself to become angry, and you can choose not to.

There are some things in life that call for anger. For those situations, the Bible teaches, "Be angry, and do not sin." (Ephesians 4:26) When it comes to your relationship with your wife, however, unleashing your anger is almost never appropriate. And giving full vent to your anger (being a fool) is never right. Rest assured, your angry spirit will bring a harvest of pain and destruction . . . and is responsible for many divorces.

*Hey, the Bible says that Christians can divorce only for adultery.*

The foolish husband says in his heart, "I only raised my voice a little, and for good reason!" But his reason will never be good enough to win back his wife's heart. That won't be much comfort when she says goodbye and closes the door. Wives have been driven away by anger. It happens. For the woman who chooses to stay, anger drives her spirit into hiding. She may be physically present, but now she must protect herself.

There are a lot of ways to be angry. Some men have mastered the silent explosion. It may involve fewer decibels, but it's just as destructive.

And, if you have kids, your anger will annihilate your relationship with them, too, which is as it should be. The Bible says not to associate with an angry man (Proverbs 22:24).

Nothing good will ever come to your marriage from the spirit of anger. Say goodbye to it now, and save yourself from a world of trouble, a future of loneliness, and from destroying what your marriage could have been.

What do you do if you've blown it – if you've walked in anger and have hurt your wife with your harsh spirit, angry countenance, and stabbing words? Remember the Proverb about soft, kind words? Restoration follows where humility and change have happened. Soft, gentle words increase your wife's hearing capacity.

*Dear Lord,*

*I recognize the spirit of anger as completely destructive and that You have given me the power to say no to this relationship menace. Please help me to hear Your voice the next time I'm tempted to give way to anger. I desire to banish it from my relationship with my wife – to honor You and to build a relationship of trust and security with her. I pray from this day forward that I would walk in control of my spirit at all times.*

*In Jesus' name, amen.*

## Ask your wife:

"Have I shown an angry spirit toward you? How has that made you feel? I desire to be done with this sin in my life and am praying for God's help in this. Will you pray for me, too?"

# Notes

# Notes

# 13
# Listen with Sincere Interest

*Wisdom cries out to the husband, "Listen when she wants to talk to you. Listen when she wants to share her heart. Listen . . . listen . . . listen, and in so doing, you have loved."*

*Y*our wife has a great need.

She doesn't need to be listened to by the world. She doesn't need to have the ear of the local newspaper. She doesn't need her voice heard in the public square. But there is something she needs deeply: to be heard by you.

So many husbands miss this most fundamental truth. To be happy and fulfilled, wives need their husbands to listen to them . . . to listen to them talk.

For most women, it's the best foreplay – knowing

that you truly care about what she is thinking, what she is concerned about, what matters to her.

The husband who seeks to find out what his wife's day has held discovers that, a little later, she wants her body held . . . by him. That's just how it works. So, listen with genuine interest as she talks and shares about her day. Find fifteen to twenty minutes toward the end of each day and "connect." Seek her out, find out how she is feeling, ask what her day was like.

Listening says, "I love you. I love who you are and I want to know you more deeply."

Here's an insight that might help you grasp why your listening makes a deep impact: when you are talking about something, you're talking about one thing. When your wife is talking about one thing, she's talking about everything. For her, it's all connected. That's why listening with genuine interest is foreplay.

The husband who listens has listened to wisdom. He will be heard when he expresses his needs.

Listening is a great relational building power held by husbands everywhere but used by so few (the happy, very happy, few).

*Dear Lord,*

*My wife deserves someone who is intensely interested in her as a person, and I recognize listening is an important way to communicate that. I want to be a better listener. Please help me to say no to distractions and anything that keeps me from not giving her the attention she deserves. Help me to be a great listener.*

*In Jesus' name, amen.*

## ASK YOUR WIFE:

"Is there something on your mind and heart that we can talk about tonight? Tell me about your day. What were you thinking about during the day?"

# Notes

# 14

# Express Your Desire for Her

*A wife stops holding hands only because she thinks her husband doesn't want to anymore.*

A year or two after the wedding, life has a way of grinding marriage down to a functional relationship. We get the bills paid, keep the fridge stocked, and put gas in the car. Yes, we're still having sex.

But where's the fire? Where's the passion? Where's the romance – the fun of the relationship that was so much a part of the first year of marriage?

You didn't plan on the fire fizzling. But, honestly, is there more than a random spark? What happened?

Why did you stop walking up beside your wife and

slipping your hand in hers? Why is physical touch (not sexual touch) becoming more and more infrequent? One thing is certain: it's not because your wife stopped desiring to be desired. She could be seventy-five years old, but she'll always long to be cherished.

Many wives wonder if it's because they are no longer loved deeply . . . that they've become unattractive to their husbands.

When was the last time you took your wife on a walk, holding hands, just the two of you?

Your wife never stopped desiring to be desired. She's waiting to respond to your gestures of love because that's what most wives do – they respond to the overtures their husbands make. And that's why she doesn't hold hands anymore – not because she doesn't want to now, but because she's waiting for your lead.

The husband who understands that his wife's desire to be desired has never diminished, and who seeks to communicate that she is desired, will have no lack of what he desires.

ATTHEW L. JACOBSON

*Dear Lord,*

*Help me to remember that I have a responsibility to touch my wife in non-sexual as well as sexual ways and to never forget how important this is to her. In this coming week, help her to feel my deep love and care for her through the simple means of physical affection.*

*In Jesus' name, amen.*

## ASK YOUR WIFE:

"Do you like holding hands? Do we hold hands enough? When it comes to non-sexual physical touch, what makes you happy?"

# 15

# Value Her Intuition and Counsel

*The heart of the man who spurns his wife's counsel will be pierced through with many sorrows, but he who recognizes the value of his wife's intuition is wise.*

*Y*our wife is a gift . . . a gift from God to you. Even so, many husbands fail to recognize her unique benefit to the marriage.

How often your wife has a different perspective than you. Same facts, same circumstances, but she has an appraisal at odds with yours. Frustration sets in. Yet again, you feel she is opposing you.

The unwise, inexperienced (often prideful) husband

sees this as a challenge, a threat to his leadership.

You think, *Why is she contradicting me? Can't she see this is a great opportunity?* Or, *He's a great guy. I can't understand why she's against him becoming our business partner.*

We husbands can be so sure of our own perspective, so convinced of our "rightness" that we determine to soldier on with our plans. We won't allow our wives to rain on our parades. No, sir! We know a good situation when we see it.

Has that ever happened in your marriage? And then what happened? You proceeded with the decision, running over the top of your wife's caution and concern, only to discover that, well, she was right. Lots of grief and money could have been spared if we would just learn to respect her unique gift of insight, intuition, and wisdom.

Perhaps you haven't yet experienced this. Your opportunity is coming.

God gave her to you for that very purpose. She completes you. You're smart. So is she. You have insight, but so does she. It was given to her to bless you, to balance those areas of blindness every husband has. Embrace the blessing God intends for you through your wife. Listen to her wisdom.

*Dear Lord,*

*My wife is an amazing gift from You. Please help me to hear Your voice in her different perspective. Please help me to understand that You have given her to me in order that I might have a wise counselor at my side. She deserves to feel valued and needed. I pray that in the coming weeks I would communicate those things clearly to her by valuing her thoughts, insights, perspective, and counsel.*

*In Jesus' name, amen.*

## ASK YOUR WIFE:

"Do you feel that I listen to and value your opinions and advice? We won't always agree, but what can I do to give you confidence that I am truly listening and seriously considering your perspective in the next decision we have to make?"

# Notes

# 16

# Remain Faithful with Your Eyes

*She walks in beauty*
*whose husband reserves his gaze for only her.*

Wives can spot their husband's wandering eye from the back of a galloping horse at one hundred yards – they can feel it in their bones. And when a wife notices her husband's eyes wandering, she gets a sick feeling in her stomach.

*Doesn't he think I'm pretty anymore?*

*Is he losing interest in me?*

*I don't measure up.*

*How can I compete with that younger woman?*

Every lustful, wayward glance is like a mini-betrayal of your wife. Over time, you can remove the "mini" designation. It's a betrayal. Are these the thoughts you want to engender in your wife through your behavior?

Where did you look this week?

Did you honor your wife with your eyes?

Oh, you may never look at the women in bras and panties at the Victoria-Doesn't-Have-Any-Secrets store when your wife is in the car. That would hurt her feelings and would, well, just be wrong.

When you're walking down a busy street and a beautiful woman is headed your way, do you look? Do you stare?

How about when you're alone? Who are you when no one is looking? Who are you when she won't find out? Fact: who you are when no one is looking is who you are.

You're hardly unique. Nothing is more natural to the flesh of a man than to want to take the second look. Our flesh is sinful. It's as simple as that. But as a Christian man, you have full power and authority to say no to your fleshly impulses.

The first look is usually unavoidable in this culture. But then you have a choice, and where is that choice taking you? Are you choosing to take a second, longer look?

Don't tell yourself you're a victim. Don't tell yourself you can't help it. Those are lies. Choosing to look is a choice – every time.

The man who makes a covenant with his eyes fills his wife with confidence and security.

Honor your wife with your gaze. Reserve it only for her and her beauty will radiate, reflecting back to you the love that you prove by your single-mindedness.

*Dear Lord,*

*Nothing comes more naturally to my flesh than to allow my eyes to linger over other women. But I want to honor You and to honor my wife. I deeply desire that she feel special and that she never has to compete with what this world has to offer. Please help me to walk in the freedom and power You have given me to control my flesh — to oppose the impulses to look at someone in a way that would dishonor my wife. Help me give my wife the confidence that comes from trusting that I seek no other beauty than hers.*

*In Jesus' name, amen.*

## SAY TO YOUR WIFE:

"I want you to know that I am completely single-minded when it comes to you. I commit to you that my eyes will never wander. Please don't worry that I will ever lust after other women. My gaze is only, ever, and always for you."

# Notes

# 17

# Care for Her Heart Through the Day

*The foolish man ignores his wife through the day and expects a warm welcome at night. All he will receive is the back of a frigid shoulder.*

It's early in the morning and you're leaving for work. Your wife is going to work, too. Either she is headed out the door to her job or she's working hard at home. Either way, you give each other a quick kiss good-bye and the day begins.

Only, you've been thinking how great it would be to go to bed early. It's been a few days . . . *Yeah, tonight we'll turn in early, and I'm looking forward to that!*

You're thinking about it all day as the hours pass.

Then you come home, distracted with the pressures of your day. You take a call or two, eat dinner, try to hurry things along and indicate to your wife how you'd like the evening to end, but she's not interested. Not tonight.

*How frustrating! I've only been thinking about this for the past twelve hours!*

At least one of you was thinking about it.

Your wife has already put in a full day, pouring out, giving. When a husband continually springs his desires on his wife at the end of the day, without cultivating the relationship, she feels it's just another opportunity for someone to get something from her.

How do you transform this "taking" into a "giving" that you both enjoy?

It starts with your perspective. Are you planning on "getting" something from your wife? Wrong move. She loves giving, but she doesn't love being used. Know the difference.

You have the power to make everything different. And it's so simple.

When you part in the morning, look into her eyes and say, "I hate to leave you! Looking forward to seeing you tonight," and she will hear, *I love you and will be thinking of you when I'm away.*

You could make a habit of texting or calling her at least once during the day, for no other reason than you want to check in, to see how her day is going.

"Hey babe, how's your day going? Just wanted to hear

your voice."

She will hear, *I love you and have been thinking about you.*

When you meet up at the end of the day, you could offer a warm, enthusiastic greeting.

"Hey beautiful, I've been waiting all day to see that smile."

She will hear, *I love you and my heart was here, with you, all day.*

You could express sincere gratitude when your wife makes dinner.

"That smells fantastic! I'm so lucky you're my wife." (A hug from behind wouldn't hurt either, and then ask if there's anything you could do to help.)

She will hear, *I love you and appreciate the gifts you give.*

In the first scenario (sadly, the most common experience of many wives), all she hears is, *Hey, I want sex from you tonight.*

In the second scenario, she's been hearing a sincere, *I love you and am thinking about you*, all day long.

Mark and learn: warm, sincere, loving words throughout the day stoke hot fires when evening falls.

The first guy is closing his wife's heart by degrees. The wise husband *opens* her heart by degrees, so coming together in the evening isn't one person taking from another but two people giving to each other.

And when it comes to marriage, givers always get more than takers.

*Dear Lord,*

*I pray my wife never feels used by me. Give me the understanding and presence of mind to love her in all the ways that make her feel valued, so when we come together at night, it's two people coming to enjoy one another and not just me coming to get what I want.*

*In Jesus' name, amen.*

## Ask your wife:

Fill in the blank: "I feel most loved by you through the day when you _____."

# Notes

Notes

# 18

# She's Your Lover, Not Your Maid

*Leaving wet towels or dirty laundry around for your wife to pick up is the same as hanging a sign around her neck that says, "I think of you as the maid."*

It's not disrespectful for a three-year-old to leave his dirty underwear on the bathroom floor for mommy to pick up.

But, you're not three.

And she isn't your mommy.

Question: how many wives enjoy their husbands treating them like the hired help?

Oh, right . . . zero.

There are many ways husbands can disrespect their wives, but one of the most annoying for many women is what is communicated by a husband who can't be bothered to pick up his shower towel, walk four feet to the rack, and hang it up. And then there are the socks . . . and . . .

Not your issues? How about leaving shaving stubble in the sink or dribbles on the toilet? Do you expect her to clear your plate after dinner?

What is the core issue with all of these habits?

Being a gentleman.

And respect for others is the core of being a gentleman. Many men treat their wives in ways they would never treat a stranger.

In every marriage, the details will look a little different, but the issue is critical for those striving to have a great marriage. Are you a gentleman when it comes to your wife?

What if the treatment were reversed? How would you then feel? Respected? Valued?

Never did the words of Jesus apply more aptly than in the day-to-day function of marriage: "Do unto others [your wife!] as you would have them [her!] do unto you." (Matthew 7:12, paraphrased)

Are you treating your wife like a maid, or are you treating her like the princess you married?

Did you know that when socks were invented, it was immediately and universally decided by wives everywhere that their husbands picking up socks and putting them in the dirty clothes hamper was synonymous with saying, "I Love You!"?

*Dear Lord,*

*There's nothing easier than taking for granted all the great things my wife does for me. From this day forward, I want to change my perspective and not slip into this selfish thought pattern. Please help me to demonstrate to her how much I value her by not treating her like the hired help. Help me to be mindful of thoughtful ways I can act toward her that reflect my love and respect for her.*

*In Jesus' name, amen.*

## ASK YOUR WIFE:

"What three habits do you wish I would begin so that you don't feel like the hired help?"

Notes

Notes

# 19
# The Grass Is Not Greener...Over There

*Where there is no will to water and fertilize,
the grass will always seem greener on the other side
of the fence. But it's never about the other side.*

Last year our lawn was a lush, dark green, but this year the color has faded, and brown patches have appeared.

Here's the thing. Grass isn't green because it's grass; it's green because it's watered and fertilized. Even the most beautiful, lush lawn will turn brown from neglect.

Marriages are the same. Have you ever hit a dry zone? Have you felt the health of your marriage diminishing by degrees?

We can find ourselves in seasons of change, seasons of challenge, seasons that demand our time and attention more than normal. There are seasons that make us tired, and they take our hearts, our marriages, into the gray zone.

It's dangerous ground for a man. It's here temptation strikes . . . a look across the fence and, *wow!* That grass looks so much greener.

It's not that there is something fundamentally wrong with the fact that the two of you are married. You've made mistakes, but your marriage is not a mistake. God doesn't make mistakes.

Just like a brown lawn, you've hit a dry patch because you haven't been giving your marriage the nutrients – the time and investment – it requires.

It's easy to look at a happy couple and conclude, *They just got lucky. Marriage is easy for them.*

It's a lie. That couple's marriage is a verdant, green field because they've made the investment. They've focused on their marriage and have stayed committed through the challenging times.

Anything great takes commitment and work. Marriage is no exception. Instead of telling yourself you just got dealt a tough hand in marriage and then resorting to looking at the greener grass on the other side of the fence, how about taking responsibility and embracing the truth?

You, too, can have a great marriage, if you are willing to stay committed, to work at it, and to mature and grow as a person. These are the very things everyone enjoying a great marriage has done and continues to do.

The fence is there for a reason – to keep out what

should not be there and to keep in what should remain. The grass isn't greener because it is on the other side of the fence. The grass is greener where it has been fertilized and watered well.

If you find yourself in a dry season and the "grass" of your marriage is showing some brown patches, it's time to refocus and make a priority of the most important human relationship you'll have this side of heaven.

Do this, and you'll be amazed how quickly the "grass" will dazzle with a deep, vibrant green.

*Dear Lord,*

*Thank You for giving me the strength to stand strong and remain single-minded, even in the face of temptation. Help me never to allow my marriage to become dry and dying like a neglected lawn. I pray my heart will never wander from Your best for me — the wife You have graciously given to me. The grass I'm standing on is my responsibility — help me to never deviate from that truth.*

*In Jesus' name, amen.*

## ASK YOUR WIFE:

"If our marriage were a lawn, would you say it is green and lush or brown and withering? If green and lush, what one thing do you think we're doing well that keeps it that way? If brown and withering, what is one thing (okay, more than one!) I can do to 'add water' immediately?"

Notes

# Notes

# 20

# Banish Bitterness Against Her

*Allowing oneself to become bitter in marriage*
*is like jumping off a bridge*
*and expecting another person to die.*

When living so closely to another human being, someone is bound to get hurt. It's what we do as humans in our imperfect ways. We don't mean to – okay, sometimes we do. But, intentional or not, at some point, we hurt each other.

What do you do when your wife hurts you? Men often don't think of it as "hurt." It's more like what she does that makes you angry. What do you think about? Do you mull it over in your mind over and over? Do you allow the hurt to turn into anger?

Incidents from months or years back can stay as fresh in our minds as the day they happened. Maybe the hurt was never dealt with. Maybe it was never accounted for. And it still *really* bugs you.

This is how bitterness in marriage finds a foothold in your heart. Once that foothold has been secured, bitterness grows and grows. The irony of bitterness is that your wife often has no idea about what is eating away at you. For months, the bitterness festers without her knowledge and then one day – boom! The right set of circumstances and it all comes out in a seething, destructive flow.

Bitterness does more than just destroy the relationship between you and your wife. It destroys *you*, from the inside. Your spirit shrivels from the poison that has become more fetid by the day.

Bitterness, like so many other things in marriage, can be handled in a very straightforward manner. You can choose (you must choose) to say no to bitterness.

Decide that you will let "it" go. Choose not to be bitter. Don't give a foothold to the poisonous root that will corrupt your heart and destroy your marriage.

Maybe you've not had cause to be bitter at your wife. Marriage has a way of providing opportunities. Choose, before you get to that milestone in marriage, not to allow a root of bitterness to grow between you and the one you love.

*Dear Lord,*

*I'm sure I've given my wife reasons to become bitter, and I know there are things that are bugging me — things that could encourage a root of bitterness to grow in our marriage. I reject that kind of thinking right now! Please take from me any inclination I have to dwell on things and become bitter about them. You've given me the power. Now help me to walk in the Spirit and use that power to refuse any pattern of negative thinking or bitter spirit toward my wife.*

*In Jesus' name, amen.*

# TELL YOUR WIFE:

"I have a heart that has the potential to grow bitter over some things in our marriage. But, I have asked God to work on my heart and I would prize your prayers for my heart as well. In addition to this, I want to tell you three things right now that I love about our marriage . . . ."

Notes

# 21
# Guard Your Mouth

*When tensions mount in marriage conflict, hold
your tongue until God has a hold on your heart.*

Two good people: you and your wife. You get along great
and enjoy each other's company. For the most part, you
have a great time together.

And then there are the other times . . .

Every once in a while, she really gets under your skin,
and the fire flares, but it's the wrong kind of fire between
spouses: destructive, anger-induced fire.

Flamethrowers – that's what many couples become in
these moments. He gives a blast and then she returns fire.

In your next "moment" there's something you need to
do, immediately:

Shut up.

That's right, SHUT UP. Intense moments are perfect for saying the thing you didn't mean, the thing that causes so much pain and mop-up later. The sharp tongue is every bit as effective as the sharpest knife. You can count on those cuts going deep.

We rarely regret what we didn't say in the moment of emotional intensity.

When tempers flare, you're walking in the flesh – your sinful flesh – and you'll not get any help from that source for proceeding in a healthy, productive manner. In fact, there's little in marriage that must be discussed in moments of frayed, uncontrolled emotion.

It's best to choose silence in the tense moment, to give you and your spouse some distance from the heat. You can agree to talk about it later, when you have control of your spirit.

When the temperature rises, it's time to be quiet – unless you're one of those men who fights with silence. (Silence is just as aggressive as the frontal assault and makes your wife crazy with anger. If that's you, you need to stop using silence as a club to beat her with.)

God always gives you the grace for everything He calls you to walk through, including the current disagreement with your spouse. Wise husbands know they don't need to say their piece "right now," when they're in the worst frame of mind to say it with love. So shut up, back up, pray up, and make up – but, definitely stop talking, *now!*

*Dear Lord,*

*I don't always need to get the last word. I don't always have to win the argument. I know the impulse to do so is caused by pride, nothing more. The next time I'm tempted to say things in the emotion of the moment, please restrain me. Help me have Your mind and the self-discipline to guard my mouth from careless words and sinful comments. I pray that my spirit would be under the control of Your Holy Spirit so that, even in intense moments, I don't give offense and can remain calm with a gentle manner.*

*In Jesus' name, amen.*

## ASK YOUR WIFE:

"Have I said anything in anger in the past that is sticking in your mind? Would you forgive me for those careless, hurtful words? I pledge to you that I will try not to speak careless words to you anymore – that the next time we have a disagreement, I'll either speak with a thoughtful, gentle spirit or I won't speak at all."

Notes

# 22

# When Romance Matters

*Romance before marriage often feels amazing,
but romance after the wedding day
is far more important.*

Your wife loves romance.

No, I don't know her. I don't have to. It's what you'll find at the core of a woman's heart.

Sadly, for many wives, not long after the honeymoon, the romantic overtures from their husband dwindle and stop altogether.

She doesn't say much about it – doesn't want to be a nag. She's given a few hints here and there, and then she just gives up. But somewhere in her heart, she still silently wishes her husband would be romantic – not just sexual – with her.

Most married men are about as comfortable with

romance as the guy holding an angry porcupine in his lap.

*I'm just not very romantic. I don't know what to do.*

Really? I have a question for you. Between your honeymoon and now, when did you get a frontal lobotomy? Because, prior to marriage, you were pretty creative in expressing your love for your wife. So what has happened?

Being romantic means putting yourself out there, like you did before you were married. You give her a card that says, "I Love You Forever." You slow dance to a romantic song with the lights low. You offer a long, slow back rub. You know what she would like.

For those of you who are out of touch and don't know what is romantic to your wife, there's a neat trick you can use to find out: study her.

Her heart for romance may be atrophied from years of neglect, but it's still there. A wise and loving husband wants his wife to enjoy romance . . . from him.

*Dear Lord,*

*So often I have good thoughts and intentions toward my wife, but I allow the busyness of life to crowd them out and just carry on with the next pressing priority, forgetting she needs my romantic attention. Please help me to always remember my wife desires to be romanced just as much as when we were first married. Help me to truly bless her by showing her my softer, romantic side on a regular basis.*

*In Jesus' name, amen.*

## ASK YOUR WIFE:

"What are some of the most romantic moments we have ever shared together?" (And then, start creating more of those moments, regularly!)

Notes

# 23
# The Only Opinion That Matters

*The wise husband understands that when she asks for his opinion about her new dress, new hairstyle, or new shoes, it's a veiled desire that he declare her beautiful.*

You were either raised right or you learned in the school of hard knocks. Be logical. Be straightforward. Be honest.

Then you got married and this time-tested wisdom was not always helpful anymore. When your wife gets a new dress, a new hairstyle, or a new pair of shoes are three of those times.

She's not looking for your honest assessment.

Because it's not about the dress, the shoes, or the hair. It's about her. It's about how she feels. And it doesn't matter if she's 26, 46, or 76 – the biggest part of how she feels is based on what you think about her.

Everywhere your wife turns, the voices of society are tearing her down.

*You're too thin, too fat, too tall, too short, too old, not pretty enough, not stylish enough . . .*

All she wants to know is that you think she looks fantastic.

So the next time she demurely asks, "Well, what do you think of this dress?"

Your answer is, "Babe, you look awesome in that dress. In fact, you make that dress look stunning."

It's up to you to defy every other voice in society with your enthusiastic praise. Leave the analysis to the post-game commentator on TV.

And, to be really on point, don't wait for her to ask. Beat her to the moment. As soon as she shows up with her new hairstyle, then . . . you go, boy!

*Dear Lord,*

*It's obvious to me that society is no friend of my wife's sense of worth and self-esteem. In the coming week, help me to think regularly of how I can speak worth, beauty, and value into her heart. Help me not only to see her this way but to help her to see how much You love and value her, too – that her true worth is based on Your deep love for her.*

*In Jesus' name, amen.*

## TELL YOUR WIFE:

Tell your wife how much you like some of the recent clothing and shoe purchases she has made, emphasizing how beautiful she is with them – and without them!

Notes

# 24
# Everyday Love in Everyday Lives

*The wise husband knows that grand gestures and lavish gifts can never replace attentiveness.*

*H*e was a workaholic – and a sportaholic when he wasn't working. And then there was his beloved restoration project of a '65 Mustang. Months went by of leaving early, working late, and working on his golf swing on the weekend. She waited patiently for him to engage, to connect, but hope was lost somewhere between the latest triumph at work and his team going to the Super Bowl.

He sensed she was feeling a little (he has no idea) passed over.

The expensive bracelet was nice. The cruise was nice.

The big party was nice. But they weren't "him" and, there's no substitute – none – for "him." It's a distinction lost on the foolish husband.

Many men think that after neglecting one's wife for months at a time, compensation can be made up by making "the big move." But it never works. Even though she's enjoying sitting on the deck of the cruise ship sipping a piña colada, she knows she's being bribed.

She doesn't want to be bribed.

She wants to be loved.

And love is about relationship.

And you can't have a relationship with a reclining deck chair somewhere on the high seas.

The simpleton pursues his own interests but tells himself, "My wife will always be there for me." He doesn't know the secrets of her heart were spirited away from him long ago and her body is soon to follow.

The star shooting through space and the marriage of a spouse pursuing his own interests without regard to his wife are alike. They both burn brightly on their own for a short time and then, all is dark. If you take your wife for granted, sooner or later she'll be tempted to find someone who will take her for what she is . . . a woman who needs love. Maybe she'd never follow through, but no good man would ever risk it.

The quality of your love for your wife is determined for her by what you do consistently over time. No grand gesture is ever enough to make up for neglect. The valued woman will enjoy her husband's grand gestures, but she has no need of them as evidence of his love for her. That evidence is given every day in the attention he gives to her as a person, as a lover, and as a friend.

The wise husband understands that what his wife really desires is him, in full measure . . . and he gives himself to her, mind, body, and soul.

*Dear Lord,*

*Help me to remember that my wife should never have to compete with anything for my attention, time, and love — that if she ever has to, I'm walking in sin. Give me insight and understanding when she starts to feel this way, and the conviction to correct my thinking and choices that have led us there. I pray for Your protection over our marriage and ask for the continuing wisdom to lead my wife lovingly.*

*In Jesus' name, amen.*

## ASK YOUR WIFE:

"Do you feel like you are competing with anything for my time and attention right now? You should never feel that you're in a competition with anything in my life. If you've ever felt that way (or feel that way right now), please know I intend to make a change. I invite you to help me see when I begin to fall into old patterns."

Notes

Notes

# 25
## No Public Disputes

*A skunk at the picnic and the arguing couple
are alike. They bring a foul stench,
from which everyone wants to get away.*

No one, absolutely no one, is interested in the stench
brought by an openly contentious couple – even
the ones who think they're feuding discreetly. But
it never fails. Get a large group together and there he is
correcting his wife in front of everyone or pointing out
how she did "it" wrong.

Everyone tries to pretend it isn't happening but it's
unavoidable – like a skunk at the picnic.

If you never struggle with this, then a blessing on you!
For the rest: just grow up and stop inflicting your private
acrimony on others. It's wrong. It's rude. It's awkward. It's
selfish. It's thoughtless of others. And it damages your

marriage.

*Well, what am I supposed to do? We were mad at each other! Am I supposed to fake it?*

Here's what to do when you're angry with each other but in the company of others. Choose to respect other people. Choose to keep them from the knowledge of your dispute. Choose to treat each other with love in public — just as if you didn't have a disagreement. And purpose to have a great time with everyone and each other and deal with it in private. This is the way of grace and maturity.

Here's what you'll typically find when you make this choice. When it comes time to speak together privately, much of the emotion of the moment will be dissipated and you'll have a far more rational discussion than would have been earlier.

When you're angry with your wife in public, love others by not indulging yourself. Everyone comes out a winner.

*Dear Lord,*

*Help me to remember to love others with my discretion. Help me to put down my fleshly impulses to argue and create tension with comments that are negative or argumentative, especially when we are with others. Help me to walk the path of wisdom and maturity and to save disagreements for private moments with my wife.*

*In Jesus' name, amen.*

## ASK YOUR WIFE:

Ask your wife to name the last time you argued with her or made her feel attacked and demeaned in front of others. Does she think you handled it well or poorly? What will you do the next time disagreements come up in public?

# Notes

# 26
## Celebrating Her Differences from You

*The wise husband recognizes her way*
*of doing things is not wrong, just different.*

You didn't set out to belittle your wife. You didn't want her to feel small. You weren't being controlling. It's just that, well . . .

You know how the job should be done. It's pretty straightforward. You've done it many times, thought it through, and by trial and error established the best approach.

Then along comes your wife and she starts doing it all wrong. Time for a lesson. After all, you just want to help. So, you get animated, explaining how she is taking the wrong approach and how she can alter course to get things right.

For you, it's about either doing things correctly or getting it wrong – you just want it done right. Who wants to do things the wrong way?

She's not listening. Her jaw tightens, she rolls her eyes at you, and turns to walk away, saying in that frustrated half-smile something like, "Fine, I'll just let you do it your way."

This wasn't really what you had in mind, but there you are, with an extra job, all by yourself.

What happened? Is this just a case of "the prideful wife" or is this the common occurrence of "the overbearing husband"?

It's easy to convince ourselves that our way is the right way. But your way isn't always the right way. It's just *your* way. And there are a lot of other ways . . . your wife's, for instance.

Yes, sometimes there is a real need to do something only one way (putting jumper cables on the correct posts, for instance), but these situations are rare in marriage. For 99.9% of the rest of situations, choose to celebrate your wife's differences. Choose to love and respect the fact that she is a unique person who sees (and does) things differently than you do.

Question: Is your wife an intelligent woman?

*Absolutely. She's very smart.*

Here's something about intelligent people. They don't like being treated like they can't walk and chew gum at the same time. And, that's how you're making her feel when you repeatedly try to get her to do things your way.

Different isn't necessarily wrong, it's just . . . different. And it is just as legitimate as your way of doing it.

And that's a good thing.

*Dear Lord,*

*My wife is a beautiful, intelligent, wonderful, individual creation of Yours, yet there are times when I don't treat her this way. She often sees things differently than I do. Please help me to recognize that her uniqueness and different way of understanding things is Your gift to me. Help me to truly see her differences as a compliment to me and not as competition to what I want to do. Give me a spirit willing to listen and to receive her input with respect.*

*In Jesus' name, amen.*

## Ask your wife:

"What are some tasks or challenges in our daily life where we take different approaches? Do you feel that I respect your way of doing things, even if it is different than the way I do them?"

Notes

# Notes

# 27

# The Emptiness of a 50/50 Marriage

*The man who gives 50% of himself to his marriage, hoping his wife will also give 50%, ends up with 0% of what marriage was designed to give.*

Many men continue to live in the independent identity they had prior to marriage. In fact, the world encourages you to think this way . . . to see marriage as requiring a contribution of a part of your life, a part of your heart, a part of your pocket book, and a part of your time — but not more than 50%.

It's an investment that only makes sense if your wife also contributes equally. If she doesn't, the "insurance" is that you'll still have your separate, independent identity and can carry on with or without her.

This is not God's way.

The Bible proposes a different model: husbands give themselves 100% to their wives – with nothing held back. God puts it this way: "Husbands, love your wives, just as Christ also loved the church and gave Himself for her." (Ephesians 5:25)

The husband who insists on emphasizing an "even deal" or an "equal split" is dividing the marriage – strengthening the spirit of independence from each other, guaranteeing so much less than what God designed couples to enjoy.

God's way is far better. See yourself as part of a single whole that is created only when you give yourself 100% to your marriage.

*What? Won't I end up with nothing? What happens to my independence? What if she doesn't love me back in the ways I need or want? Isn't this a risky proposition – a 100% investment without knowing how much she will return?*

This is where the wisdom of God is different than the wisdom of the world. By loving her 100%, you are blessed by God for walking in obedience to His Word. And instead of losing yourself, you end up blessing yourself when you bless and love your wife.

This Bible's way of looking at marriage requires a change of mindset, a different (more accurate) way of understanding the reality of marriage.

I, me, and mine have been replaced with us, ours, and

we. There truly is just one entity after marriage. That's why the Bible says that he who loves his wife, loves himself.

Wise, truly loving husbands don't love to get. They love to bless and inspire and are blessed in return.

Love your wife 100% this week, regardless of the percentage she is putting in and you will end up enjoying the blessings of obedience to God's way of oneness in marriage.

*Dear Lord,*

*My thinking needs to change. It's so natural for me to think of myself as an individual, but You say otherwise for the married man. Help me to understand myself as only one-half of a whole that was created when I said, "I do!" Help me to communicate my commitment to oneness with my wife, in a way that my wife can feel deep in her heart.*

*In Jesus' name, amen.*

## ASK YOUR WIFE:

"Are there any times that I use *I*, *me*, and *mine* when you would rather hear me say 'us,' 'ours,' and 'we'?"

Notes

*Notes*

# 28
# Deal Properly with Offenses

*Offenses swept under the rug never stay there.*

Life moves along at a pretty fast clip. There's hardly time to deal with all the normal necessary things, let alone to find time for a little enjoyment here and there. And then there are the rough patches in the marriage – times when an offense was suffered. But life won't slow down, so we tend to sweep offenses aside, keep barreling into the continuing crisis of our schedules, don't talk about it . . . and somehow try to get back to a functional marriage.

Is it possible to grow deep and strong in marriage when this is the pattern? When we just stuff down the effects and emotions of that offense and continue on as if all is well?

No, it isn't. Offenses swept under the rug of our frenetic lives never stay there. Pretending things are okay when offenses have been left unaddressed is neither healthy, nor is it the way a mature husband oversees his relationship with his wife.

Don't ignore offenses.

Of course, you *should* overlook minor offenses and scrapes. Some husbands and wives are determined to "die on every hill," but many offenses in marriage should just be overlooked. That's what love does. Give the grace you desire to receive when you're not at your best moments. 1 Peter 4:8 says, "And above all things have fervent love for one another, for 'love will cover a multitude of sins.'"

But what about the more major offenses? What do you do if you feel you have been wounded by your wife?

Here's the irony: the Bible places the responsibility for dealing with offenses *on the wounded party*. You can read about this in Matthew 18:15. Almost seems kind of backward, doesn't it? Shouldn't the one who caused the offense attempt to make it right?

Yes, she should, if she knows she has committed the offense. But that's the nature of offenses – often we don't realize we've committed them, so it's up to the wounded spouse to speak up.

When you speak up, you must do so in an attitude of love, speak with gentleness, explain your hurt, and not expect any response from her.

Yes, that's right – expect no response.

*What? But I am the offended party! Shouldn't she be sorry and at least apologize when I bring up my offense?*

No. Christ loves us freely even when we don't "get it." You are supposed to love your wife in the same way – speak the truth in love and leave her free to respond in her own time.

As the leader of your home, it's your responsibility to make sure you have this proactive and patient attitude.

The storms of marriage don't develop character and strength of relationship; they reveal the strength of the relationship that is already there. Build that strength into the fabric of your marriage, and you'll be prepared to properly deal with what inevitably confronts every marriage at some point.

One last word: when offenses are acknowledged and forgiveness has been humbly sought and given, never, *ever* bring up that offense again. After we've repented, God doesn't throw our past sins and failures in our faces, and we should never do so to our wife. Be sure to discuss this with your wife as well. Many husbands and wives naturally default to this destructive practice, but you and your wife, learning and growing together, can grow past this immature response.

Wise prep work happens prior to the storm.

*Dear Lord,*

*It's so easy to bypass the discomfort of dealing with offenses — whether I've given them or received them. But I know, left unaddressed, they have the power to destroy. Help me to man up and deal with them — to take the responsibility of keeping communication open and not allowing the build-up of resentment in my marriage.*

*In Jesus' name, amen.*

## Ask your wife:

"Have I upset you lately in any way? Are there things that have offended you but that you've 'stuffed' . . . things that are still hurting you even though you've not said anything? Please tell me about it. I want to listen and understand and grow in this area so that I will not be as likely to upset you again."

Notes

Notes

# 29

# The Message Your Countenance Sends to Her Heart

*The schedule may prevent taking her out tonight, but that never stops the loving husband from dating her with his eyes.*

Are you mindful of your countenance? Are you aware of what you're saying with the expression on your face?

She's watching you, sensing you, experiencing you in the moment. You haven't opened your mouth, but you don't have to in order to speak volumes to her heart.

So, what are you saying with your body language and

the way you look?

A thoughtful, kind, purposeful expression sent your wife's direction will travel all the way to her heart. You have the power to impart peace to your woman, just by letting her know all is well with the two of you, with nothing more than a kind smile and a loving look.

Becoming aware of and taking responsibility for what you communicate when you're *not* speaking is part of walking in oneness. Controlling your body language is accepting that you are not some independent entity who can act independently of the woman you are sharing your life with.

Find lots of moments to say, "I love you," "I'm grateful for you," or "I think you are amazing" with your eyes. It's a great way to "date" when the weekly schedule prevents going out.

*Dear Lord,*

*I want to take responsibility for the feelings I project into the room by the look on my face. Many times, my thoughts are miles away. Help me to be aware of what I am saying to my wife through my body language and facial expressions. In the coming days, may my face reflect a positive spirit toward my beautiful wife.*

*In Jesus' name, amen.*

## ASK YOUR WIFE:

"What are the times that I appear most distracted to you? I'm trying, with God's help, to be more 'present' for you, but I want to learn a little more about when I'm not . . . ."

Notes

# 30
## For Her, It's All Connected

*The husband who only desires to enter his wife's*
*body will, at best, receive a loveless embrace.*
*The husband who desires to enter his wife's world*
*will receive more than he could have imagined.*

In a fallen world where people are out for themselves, men give relationship to get sex and women give sex to get relationship. God wants better for us. He wants our marriage relationship to be based on His Word and how He made us to walk in love with each other.

For the husband, the most important starting point with his wife is to gain an understanding of how she thinks, how she processes information. Why is it important to truly grasp this? It's because her way is completely different from yours (of course, there are exceptions).

You compartmentalize everything: the intense business

deal, the earthquake that killed thousands, the house fire your friends sustained, your mother's cancer, your son's baseball game, the sermon on Sunday – everything.

For your wife, it's all connected – all of it. It's the totality of her thoughts/feelings/experiences of her day (and often preceding days).

Did you catch that? **For her, it's all connected – everything:** the events of her day, how she's feeling physically, that difficult conversation she had with a teacher at school, the cold her second child has, the intimate time you both hope to have tonight, the overdue house payment, the neighbor's call about their stray cat, the great article on autism she read while eating lunch, the misunderstanding she had with her sister over the phone, and the news report of the war in the middle east where thousands were killed.

It's connected . . . it really is. It's all one giant ball of string. And don't try to unravel it just because you believe some of those things shouldn't be in there. In fact, it's best if you don't even touch that ball right now. Just listen.

Her emotional, spiritual, and physiological wiring handles a major current that assimilates and coalesces into her state of mind.

Therefore, when you meet her desire to be heard, known, and understood, you are creating desire in her for you.

Wise husbands make a study of their wives and embrace – rather than rebel against – the differences. But be sure to keep your reasons and motives in proper priority. When your motive is to meet her needs by truly loving her in the ways that say love to her, it all comes back to you. You'd sooner hide the sun on a clear day than hide the radiant beauty of a loved wife.

He who continues to cherish continues to receive. A truly loved woman is almost impossible to out-give.

*Dear Lord,*

*I like sex. I want sex with my wife . . . often . . . (Just being honest!) But, I also desire to mature — to move far beyond merely what I want and to be a giving, not a taking husband. Help me to see that in pursuing and desiring my wife, I am creating in her the deep satisfaction that comes to a genuinely loved woman. And, when I love her in this way, she is freer to love me. It's so simple . . . and so easy to forget. Help me to grow in this area.*

*In Jesus' name, amen.*

## ASK YOUR WIFE:

With genuine interest, ask your wife about her day, what she has been thinking about, about her dreams and plans for the future. By so doing, you are learning to practice seeking her heart.

Notes

# Notes

# 31
# The Wife Who Never "Nags"

*The man who readily helps his wife around the home removes the need for her to nag.*

It's easy to complain about your wife harping on you, bugging you to do things and being a (we'd never say it out loud, would we?) . . . well . . . nag.

No woman sets out to get married and to become a nagging wife, yet why do many wives find themselves in just this position?

The real issue here isn't what your wife wants you to do. It's something much deeper than various tasks that aren't getting done. Boil it all down, and what you will find at the core of her continual badgering is the feeling of not being considered and cared for. Even if she doesn't say it, do you want your wife thinking, *He doesn't care for me . . . or care how I feel?*

A woman who doesn't feel responded to in the little things around the house doesn't feel cared for. That's why, in survey after survey, wives report that they find it very sexy to see their man helping around the house. It's not so much about the task that he is doing but that he is expressing love to her by doing the chore that was requested.

When you respond immediately to your wife's requests or just dive in and help with various chores, your wife feels cared for. This makes just about any woman feel loved and removes the impulse to badger you with requests.

*Really? Replacing that light bulb, tightening the toilet paper roll, and moving that shelf where she asked (about 1,000 times!) makes her feel I love her?*

Yes, it truly does.

Of course, every wife is different. The tasks that one wife would love help with, are the tasks another wants her husband to steer clear of. In our home, for instance, my wife doesn't want me to do the vacuuming. She prefers to do this herself, so I look for other ways to help keep the wheels on our wagon. But the principle of expressing love by helping out works in every marriage.

For most men, the easy solution to, shall we say, "the over-requesting wife," is to remove the reasons she feels compelled to constantly attempt to get your attention and help. The simple answer to the nagging wife is staring you in the face every morning when you look in the mirror.

Why not surprise her today? Why not bless her this week? Why not love her – yes, *love her* – by helping quickly when she requests your help? Or, better yet, start helping before she asks and become one of those "sexy" statistics in the surveys.

*Dear Lord,*

*If I am the reason my wife is nagging or badgering me to do things, please help me to embrace this simple, straightforward wisdom and love her by responding quickly to her requests. I pray that she will see in me an attentive, caring husband who takes delight in blessing her with a ready and willing heart to help around the home.*

*In Jesus' name, amen.*

## Ask your wife:

"What one chore do you want my help with this week? I promise, Lord willing, that I will have this done by [give a specific date], and you will not have to ask me to do it again."

*Notes*

*Notes*

# Conclusion

# Where Will You Go from Here?

*The blessings of obedience follow those who are willing to change . . . willing . . . and who follow through on what they have learned.*

I t's not enough that you have read. It's not enough that you have learned. God's best in marriage is there for you only if you yield your heart to biblical wisdom.

I pray that you will take what you have learned and apply it to the most important human relationship you will ever have. The benefits are amazing (your wife will be so happy!) but best of all, you will be walking in obedience to the Word of God, which brings the blessing of obedience both in this life and in the one to come.

God bless you on your journey of loving your wife as He taught us to love.

Dear Lord,

I lift up before Your throne the reader of this book and ask that You would give him the single-minded desire first to honor You and then to cherish his wife by loving her as Christ loved the Church and gave Himself for it. Where mercy and/ or forgiveness is needed, I pray that he would humbly offer it to, or receive it from, his wife.

Please bring peaceful, deeply passionate, committed love to this man and his wife. Please protect his marriage from the deceit and lies of the enemy, from the compromises of the world, and from his own flesh that works against your best in his life. Give this man the spirit and will to follow through on what he has learned and bless his marriage for Your glory.

In Jesus' name, amen.

Notes

# Notes

# Notes

Notes

# Notes

Notes

Notes

# Notes

Notes

*Notes*

*Notes*

Notes

I'd like to invite you to join me at **MatthewLJacobson.com** where we discuss marriage, parenting, Church, and culture.

facebook.com/matthewljacobson

instagram.com/matthewljacobson

pinterest.com/MatthewLJ

twitter.com/MLJacobson

Matthew Jacobson

I want to encourage you to visit **Club31Women.com**, a special gathering place to find inspiration and practical help in our relationships as wife, mother, homemaker, friend, and neighbor.

🄵 facebook.com/Club31Women

🄸 instagram.com/club31women

🄿 pinterest.com/Club31Women

🄓 twitter.com/LisaClub31Women

🄾 Club31Women

Also available from Matthew L. Jacobson:

LIKE YOU,
WE'RE ON A
LIFE-LONG JOURNEY
OF LEARNING TO
LOVE EACH OTHER.

100 WAYS TO
LOVE
YOUR WIFE

MATTHEW L. JACOBSON

Practical, hands-on advice you can start applying immediately - for the soon-to-be married man, as well as the "veteran" husband.

**www.LoyalArtsMedia.com**

Also available from Lisa Jacobson:

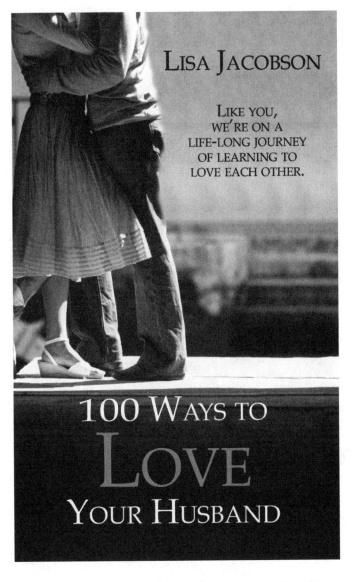

LISA JACOBSON

LIKE YOU,
WE'RE ON A
LIFE-LONG JOURNEY
OF LEARNING TO
LOVE EACH OTHER.

100 WAYS TO
LOVE
YOUR HUSBAND

God wants your marriage to be beautiful and resilient. This book offers specific, real-life instruction on how to enjoy the best marriage has to offer.

The companion to *Marriage Wisdom for Him*

Matthew L. Jacobson & Lisa Jacobson

# Marriage Wisdom

### FOR HER

## A 31 DAY DEVOTIONAL
FOR BUILDING A BETTER MARRIAGE

www.LoyalArtsMedia.com